Heaven Has Tea Parties

Michelle Post, PhD

Dedication

This book is dedicated to Annie,
I miss you and love you very much.

Proceeds from this book:

All the proceeds from the sale of this book

will be donated to the

American Parkinson Disease Association

in the memory of my mother, Annie.

http://apdaparkinson.org/

Foreword

Life has a way of tainting our vision, causing us to have a perspective that keeps us from embracing what is beautiful in the midst of painful and unthinkable circumstances. No one ever believes their life will be pillaged through Parkinson's disease; yet, as many as one million Americans and an estimated seven to 10 million people worldwide live with it—more than the total number of people diagnosed with multiple sclerosis, muscular dystrophy, and Lou Gehrig's disease. According to the Parkinson's Disease Foundation, approximately 60,000 Americans are diagnosed with Parkinson's each year, and that number does not reflect those cases that go undetected. It's not a disease that takes a life and spares the suffering of it, but one that lingers and brings sorrow and pain at every turn.

Michelle Post has lived through the tragedy of Parkinson's disease, as she watched her beloved mother helplessly succumb to it. Tempted to surrender to the anguish that comes from helplessly watching her beautiful mother face the destruction of the disease, Michelle finds herself unable to live past what she sees unfolding before her—an earthly treasure, her mother, taking on a form she'd never imagined. As she sits by and hopelessly pleads with God through drowning tears, she's given a gift—a gift of God's glory in the midst of the despair and sorrow. By the grace of God, she is given the ability to see through God's eyes and not her own. It may just be the gift you need, and Michelle wants to share that gift with you.

—Cherie Hill, *Bestselling Christian Living Author, founder of ScriptureNow.com and WriteSource Publishing Services.*

"Cream and sugar please" is the way I take my tea. I am the daughter of a beautiful woman from Newfoundland. My mom was the ninth child of twelve and grew up on the island speaking with an English accent, having tea instead of coffee, and eating scones and raisin buns. I loved having tea with my mom, just as I loved having coffee with my dad. It was our special time together. We didn't talk about anything of significance; we just enjoyed the comfort of the cup and the conversation.

One of my most favorite memories shared with my mother was having "high tea" at a quaint little restaurant, "The Secret Garden." The Cambridge Dictionary (n.d.) defines a high tea as, "a light meal eaten in the late afternoon or early evening which usually includes cooked food, cakes, and tea to drink." We had to make reservations for a "high tea" and needed to wear our Sunday best. We sat there as the wait staff brought out a carousel of English finger sandwiches and sweets. And the best sweet of all was an English scone with clotted cream, raspberry jam, and lemon curd. My mouth still waters thinking about that experience.

The teas were served in fine china teapots with a cup and saucer that matched. We had our choice of the type of tea we wanted and received our very own teapot. From it, escaped the aroma of comfort. I definitely have my mother's English blood, for I love a great cup of Earl Grey—only black tea for me—with cream and sugar. A high tea is heaven on earth. My mom and I would discuss which sandwiches we liked best, and we never shared our scone with one another. They were just too good to part with, even for one bite.

I also found the name of the restaurant, "The Secret Garden," described another of my mom's favorite pastimes. She didn't have just one green thumb; she had two green hands and arms. Every Texas spring, her gardens were beautiful. Her flowerbeds were filled with perennials and annuals of every shape and color. But it was her rose bushes that were her favorite flower. She could name every species of plant she tended. I remember taking my mom to the garden shop when I lived in Texas. As I pushed the cart behind her, I was continually amazed by her knowledge of the different kinds of plants, whereas I never even knew the difference between a perennial and an annual.

I always had to laugh when she came to my home in Colorado and would ask, "Shelly, what kind of flower is that?" as she pointed to a particular flower in my garden. I would answer that it was a yellow flower, a crimson flower, or whatever color was growing at that time in my garden. I still pick the flowers for my garden by deciding on a color scheme and going with it. Who knew there is a lot more to picking the right species to grow together or the right number of plants? Not me!

I have grown up with many labels in my life: wife, sister, aunt, the baby sibling, teacher, learner, and one of the most interesting, given to me by the government—a DINK (double income no kids). But it is my newest label that I thought I'd never realize in my lifetime, "motherless daughter," which is the most painful of all. I was given this label on Tuesday, August 9, 2011, when my mother died. I don't like this label and still haven't gotten used to it.

As I sat by my mother's bed at the nursing home, the days ran into nights and the nights into days. She struggled for each breath, and though I felt like each would be her last, it was not yet to be — exactly when her last breath would occur we didn't know. While I watched each moment unfold and wondered if this would be the closing act of the scene, I could only feel hurt, loss, and sadness. I watched a once vibrant woman with beautiful brown eyes and a smile that could melt the coldest of hearts, slowly decay in front of me. *This cannot be*, I thought. *This isn't the way her life should end.* I prayed, and prayed, and prayed, but didn't find relief.

Each day brought with it the reality of what was happening—another night of no sleep and another morning of false alarms, for this was not yet to be her final moment. It was as if my family and I were rehearsing the same scene repeatedly, day after day. Our mom would make it through another day, only to begin failing around 5:30 in the morning. "Call your family," the hospice nurse would say. One by one, I would call my siblings and each would arrive shortly after the call. We then rushed to mom's side—crying, whaling, waiting, and waiting, and then she would rally. Five days passed with this same dress rehearsal, but no final performance—at least not yet.

Then we changed the scene, and for the first night since her fall, all her children departed the nursing home, leaving her with two earthly angels, Bill and Troy, her hospice nurses. Our mom completely changed the final scene on the sixth day and decided to go home on her own. We got the call from Troy, "Come quick, she is going." Although we were only 5.8 miles (15 minutes) away, Tuesday morning traffic kept us from her death scene.

As we raced those 5.8 miles, we looked up with tear-soaked eyes and paused in awestruck wonder at the beauty of the morning sunrise. Texas had been experiencing above-normal temperatures all summer and these last six days had been no different, until this one when the morning was cool. Words cannot even begin to describe the sunrise God presented that morning and we knew before we got the next call, "She is gone," that she had already left for home. We knew this, for morning was my mom's favorite time. She would fix herself a cup of tea or coffee, sit on her back porch, and watch the beautiful sunrises. And this day was to be her greatest sunrise of all.

We arrived a few minutes after the call, running through the nursing home to try to catch her, but it was too late. Her body, still warm, and a final releasing of her spirit was all that remained for a fleeting few seconds. Just as we rehearsed the scene each prior day, one by one her children arrived to say our last goodbyes. Why she couldn't or didn't want to wait for her kids, we will never know for certain.

The subsequent hours were brutal, for the tears would not stop. I had become a motherless daughter and an orphan, all in one day. My siblings and I left the room to make the calls — those dreaded telephone conversations one never wants to face. I had to tell her only living sister that her big sister had just died. And then another call, and another, and another, until all family and friends had been notified.

What I didn't realize until I returned to the room, was that our hospice nurse, Bill, had begun to prepare her body after everyone left. What a shocking site to see my mother so frail and void of life. Then Bill said to me, "In Egypt when they buried the pharaohs, they prepared the body with oils, and that is what I am going to do for your mom too." He gently straightened my mom's broken body, lovingly put cream on her arms and legs, and with extreme tenderness combed her hair back, then crossed her arms, and covered her with one of her favorite quilts. It looked like she was sleeping.

Each of my siblings and I took our private moments with her to say our final goodbyes and held her hand one last time. After we each sat with her alone, we made the call to the funeral home, but we couldn't stay to see her taken away. We gathered ourselves and headed off to make the funeral plans. It was amazing to me how God gave us the strength and courage to handle all of the administrative tasks that were required, especially for a parent—our last parent.

August 9, 2011 ended with us looking through hundreds of pictures and selecting all of our favorites of our mom. What I realized as I looked at her through the '60s to the present was that I had forgotten how beautiful she had been. Oh, my gosh, she was gorgeous! The last few years had taken a toll on her. Her body had become frail and her once beaming brown eyes had taken on a vacant look that left me feeling uneasy, because I knew she was in there but couldn't get out due to the Parkinson's and dementia. The pictures, however, brought back her beauty. The most amazing thing we discovered was that our mom smiled in every photo we had of her. That night I came across my favorite picture of her—she was standing on her back porch with peppered short hair and the most captivating smile. That was and is how I want to remember my mom—not the woman in the bed who had no life left in her eyes.

Wednesday the 10th arrived, with us continuing to make the arrangements. What an amazing blessing we discovered that day! Our mother had planned everything right down to the pillow in the casket. She had given us that gift! We only had to make two decisions; the rest had been done for us. That night, we returned to my brother's home and I tried to sleep, but sleep would not come for me.

I replayed each moment of every hour I had spent by my mom's side and prayed that she knew how much I loved her—how deeply I would miss her. I couldn't close my eyes without seeing my mom lying in that bed with her vacant eyes, gaunt cheeks, and a frail frame. The image was etched in my brain. *Where was the beautiful woman from the pictures?* As I struggled to sleep and fought with this image I could not seem to erase, God began to ease my mind and spoke to me, *"You are seeing your mother through your eyes, but I want you to see her through Mine."*

As God helped me see through His eyes, I began to envision that vibrant woman once again. I saw her in stunning colors with angelic radiance that emitted from her. I watched her walk through the most majestic gardens as she held my Father's hand. He was showing her around, and she was meeting family and friends for a high tea. As she sat there with my dad, they laughed and smiled, drinking their tea and eating scones. When it was time for her to leave, she turned to me, waved, and gave me a big smile. "I will love you forever," she said as she turned to go.

I had watched my mom die through my eyes, not through God's eyes. I couldn't see the beauty of her new life, only the pain of the current situation. I know God provided me this opportunity to see my mom through His eyes so I could find comfort and know that she is in eternal glory, not the fading image of life. I know I will see my mom again, and when I do, we will sit in "The Secret Garden" and share a cup of tea.

But now, for a brief moment,
the LORD our God has been gracious
in leaving us a remnant and giving us
a firm place in his sanctuary,
and so our God gives light to our eyes
and a little relief in our bondage.

Ezra 9:8 NIV

Psalm 23

The L ORD *is* my shepherd;
I shall not want.
He makes me to lie down in green pastures;
He leads me beside the still waters.
He restores my soul;
He leads me in the paths of righteousness
For His name's sake.
Yea, though I walk through the valley
of the shadow of death,
I will fear no evil;
For You *are* with me;
Your rod and Your staff, they comfort me.
You prepare a table before me
in the presence of my enemies;
You anoint my head with oil;
My cup runs over.
Surely goodness and mercy shall follow me
All the days of my life;
And I will dwell in the house of the L ORD
Forever.

(NKJV)

About the Author

Dr. Michelle Post has a broad career that spans more than 30 years in business and technology. She has been teaching in both corporate and now academia on a variety of subjects that include generational studies, social media, leadership, organizational development, human resource development, marketing, team building, and professional development. Dr. Post is also noted for her energetic and demonstrative speaking skills, unorthodox ideas for solutions to problems and possessing a high level of behavioral versatility, providing the flexibility and responsiveness needed to handle a variety of situations or work environments. Michelle Post, Ph.D. can be reached at:
mpost.phd@gmail.com
or www.ReachYourPotential.info.